© Macmillan Education Limited 1988
© BLA Publishing Limited 1988

First published 1988

Published by
MACMILLAN EDUCATION LTD
Houndmills, Basingstoke, Hampshire RG21 2XS
and London
Companies and representatives
throughout the world

Designed and produced by BLA Publishing Limited,
Swan Court, East Grinstead, Sussex, England.

Also in LONDON · HONG KONG · TAIPEI · SINGAPORE · NEW YORK

A Ling Kee Company

Illustrations by Anna Hancock; Sallie Alane Reason and Linda Thursby/Linden Artists
Colour origination by Waterden Reproductions
Printed in Hong Kong

British Library Cataloguing in Publication Data

Burgess, Jan
    The heart and blood. — (How our bodies
    work). — (Macmillan world library)
    1. Blood — Circulation — Juvenile literature
    I. Title   II. Steele, Philip   III. Series
    612'.1   QP103

ISBN 0-333-45960-1

Photographic credits

t = top b = bottom l = left r = right

cover: Trevor Hill

4 Science Photo Library; 6 The Hutchison Library; 7 Vivien Fifield; 8*t* Royal College of Physicians; 8*b* Science Photo Library; 9 Ann Ronan Picture Library; 10 Science Photo Library; 13 J. Allan Cash; 14 Biophoto Associates; 15 Vision International; 16 S. & R. Greenhill; 17*t* Science Photo Library; 17*b* S. & R. Greenhill; 19 J. Allan Cash; 20 Biophoto Associates; 21*t*, 21*b*, 22 Science Photo Library; 23 S. & R. Greenhill; 26 Frank Lane Picture Agency; 26*t* Vision International; 27*b* S. & R. Greenhill; 29*t* Vision International; 29*b* LAT Photographic; 31 Science Photo Library; 32*l*, 32*r* Biophoto Associates; 33*t* J. Allan Cash; 33*b*, 34, 35*t*, 35*b* Science Photo Library; 36 St Bartholomew's Hospital; 37 Dr T. Korn/ Ysbyty Gwynedd; 38, 39*t*, 39*b* Science Photo Library; 42 S. & R. Greenhill; 44*t* ZEFA; 44*b* Vision International; 45 S. & R. Greenhill

Note to the reader
In this book there are some words in the text which are printed in **bold** type. This shows that the word is listed in the glossary on page 46. The glossary gives a brief explanation of words which may be new to you.

Contents

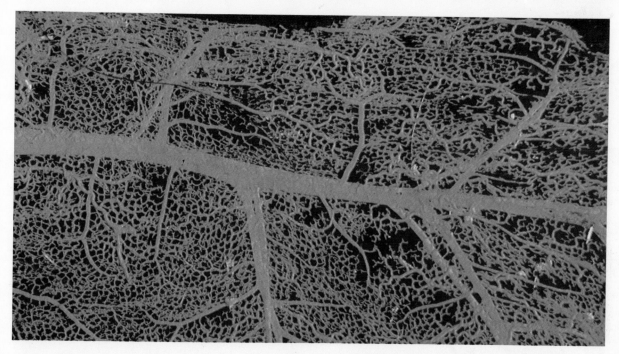

Introduction

In the middle of your chest is your **heart**. It started beating when you were still inside your mother. This was about seven months before you were born. Your heart has kept beating since then whether you have been asleep or awake. It will go on beating until you die. The heart does not always beat at the same speed. In an adult, the heart beats 60 to 80 times a minute. A child's heart beats 80 to 100 times a minute. Your heart never gets tired.

Keeping us alive

The bones called the **ribs** make a strong cage around your heart. The central bone or **sternum** helps to protect it as well. An adult's heart is about the size of a clenched fist. A child's heart is smaller. It grows as the child grows.

The heart pumps a red liquid called **blood** to every part of the body. It pushes the blood from the roots of your hair to the tips of your toes and back again. Blood carries vital substances to every part of your body. If any part of the body is cut off from the supply of blood, it dies. It is vital for the heart to keep on pumping blood.

When parts of your body are very busy, they need extra blood. The heart then has to work faster to pump the extra blood to that area. The heartbeat gets faster. Instead of beating 70 times a minute, an adult's heart may go up to 100 times a minute.

A child's heart can beat even faster. For example, when you ride your bicycle uphill, you get out of breath and your legs feel tired. Your leg muscles need more blood than usual. Your heart has to pump faster to supply that extra blood. You can feel your heart thumping in your chest. Once you have reached the top of the hill you soon get your breath back. Your heartbeat slows down to normal again.

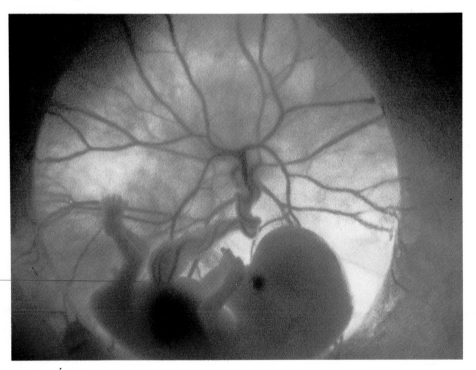

◄ Blood keeps us alive even before we are born. It helps babies grow when they are still inside their mother. The heart sends blood to every part of the baby's body.

Lessons to learn

This book explains how the heart works and why blood is so important. It also explains how you can look after your heart.

Our hearts usually go on working without a problem all our lives. Sometimes things go wrong. Heart disease is a growing problem in some countries. Doctors are finding out new things all the time about why the heart does not always work properly. They know already that people should take care of their hearts when they are young. If they do they may prevent heart disease later on.

▼ You can feel your heart beating on the left hand side of your chest when you are out of breath. It works together with the other parts of your body. The heart keeps us alive by pumping blood through the body.

Birds need a lot of energy in order to fly, which means that their bodies need a rapid supply of blood. Birds therefore have hearts which are quite large for their body size, and which beat very fast.

Different kinds of animals have various ways of pumping blood around their bodies. Each system has developed to suit the needs of the animal. The human heart has developed to suit the kind of life we lead.

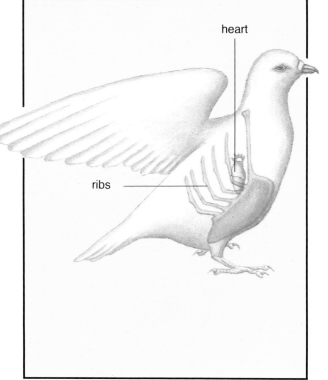

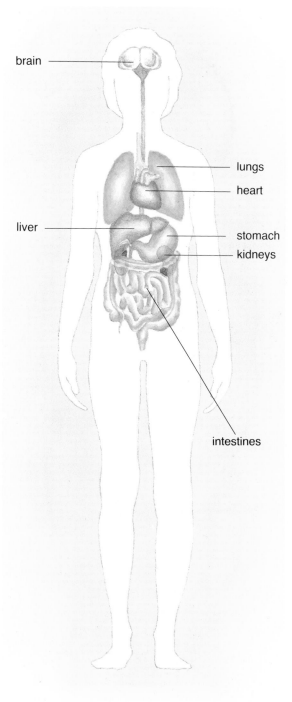

The first healers

▼ A Buddhist monk treats a snake bite. Modern scientists have told us how the body works and have found many wonderful cures for illness. However, in many parts of the world the same healing methods are used that have been tried for thousands of years.

Long ago, there were no doctors or nurses to look after people when they became ill. There were no books with good advice. People could only do simple things to make the sick feel better. They might wash a cut or make a soothing drink from plants. It was hard to understand why some people got better with this treatment while others did not. Many people believed that it was bad magic that made them ill, or good magic that made them better.

Early doctors

The first doctors used all kinds of things to make medicines. The medicines were made from plants, minerals, insects and animals like mice and frogs. Some doctors believed that if a plant had heart-shaped leaves it must be good for the heart.

From about 2500 years ago, doctors began to work out new ideas about how to

treat patients. In ancient Egypt there were different doctors for different parts of the body. The most famous doctor in ancient Greece was Hippocrates. He is often called the father of modern medicine. He believed, quite wrongly, that the veins carried air around the body. He also believed that there were fluids called **humours** in the body. If they were not in the right amounts they caused disease. One of these humours was blood.

Another famous Greek doctor, named Galen, cut open, or **dissected**, the bodies of dead animals to study them. He wrote many books. Doctors followed his ideas for hundreds of years. We now know that some of the things Galen taught were wrong. For example, he thought that the heart heated up the blood. He also thought blood flowed backwards and forwards through the body like the tide on a beach.

► The first doctors knew that the heart and blood were important, but they understood little about how the body worked. Their patients often died.

Searching for the truth

Doctors in other parts of the world were also finding out more about how the body works. Early Chinese doctors knew that blood travels round the body. They also checked the health of their patients by listening to their heartbeats. This was long before such ideas were tried out in Europe.

Vesalius proved that many of the old ideas about medicine were wrong. He was a doctor and teacher who lived in Italy 400 years ago. He dissected dead human bodies and found out that the blood is carried through the body in tubes.

Hearts and love

Many of the ideas that doctors had about how the body works seem odd to us now. One idea was that different parts of the body could make us have different feelings. The heart was supposed to control our feelings of love. Even now, people still connect the heart with the idea of love. People talk about having a broken heart when they are very unhappy, and some people send Valentine's Day cards, with pictures of hearts on, to people they love. However, people today know that the heart is really just another part of the body.

Finding out

Nobody understood why the heart and blood were very important. When someone was ill, they were sometimes given the blood of animals to drink. In some cases, people were made to bleed by doctors. The blood lost by **blood-letting** was supposed to be replaced by a new magic substance.

In 1578 a man named William Harvey was born. Harvey was the first to say that the heart was a pump. He found out that it pushed the blood along tubes called **blood vessels**. He noticed that some vessels take blood away from the heart. Others bring it back again. He also noticed that there are tiny doors called **valves** in some of the blood vessels. They only open one way. Harvey had discovered that blood flows around the body all the time. This is called the **circulation** of the blood.

▲ William Harvey was a doctor at St Bartholomew's Hospital in London. He was the first person to explain how blood travelled around the body. Here he is shown talking to King Charles I.

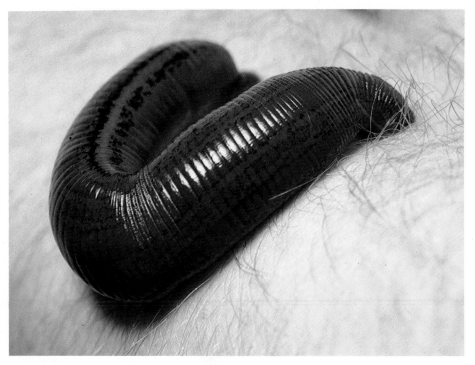

◀ Doctors kept water creatures called leeches specially for blood-letting. The leeches were put on the patient's skin. They sucked out some of the patient's blood. When the leeches were full, they dropped off. They could be used again later.

More discoveries

Harvey's work made it easier to understand how the heart and blood work. Some doctors tried taking blood from one animal and giving it to another animal. This is called a blood **transfusion**. Then they tried transfusing blood from animals to people. These experiments often ended in the death of the patients. Soon it was against the law in Europe to transfuse blood. It was not until 100 years ago that doctors found out there are different kinds of blood. Only certain kinds can mix.

Anton van Leeuwenhoek was a Dutchman born in 1632. He was one of the first people to use a **microscope**. A microscope makes things look larger. Leeuwenhoek looked at blood through his microscope. He saw that it is made of tiny bits. These tiny bits are blood **cells**. Being able to look at blood so closely helped scientists learn more about what it does.

▼ The first microscopes did not look like the ones doctors use today. Anton van Leeuwenhoek made some which could make tiny objects look 300 times larger. Doctors could now examine blood and see what it was made up of.

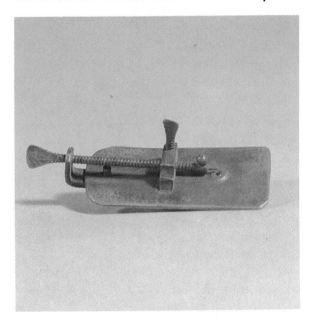

Hearing the heart

We cannot see inside our bodies, but we can hear what is going on. René Laënnec was a French doctor who lived nearly 200 years ago. He was looking after a girl who he thought might have heart disease. He needed to listen to her heartbeat, so he rolled up a newspaper. He put one end to his ear and the other to her chest. He found that he could hear her heartbeat quite clearly. Laënnec went on to make a wooden tube or **stethoscope**. Doctors today use stethoscopes, based in Laënnec's idea, for listening to their patients' hearts.

▲ This is how Leewenhoek used his microscope. The lens was raised to the eye. The position of the object could be adjusted with the screw.

Around the body

Your body is made up of millions of cells. Cells of the same kind grow together and build up into **tissue**. Different kinds of tissue make up our skin, muscles, nerves and the main parts of our bodies called **organs**. Whatever kind of tissue it is, it needs a gas called **oxygen** and fuel to stay alive.

The food you eat is the fuel that keeps your body going. Your body breaks the food up into very tiny pieces. These tiny food pieces are separated into useful substances called **nutrients**, and into waste.

Blood takes the nutrients and many other important things to every part of the body. Blood also carries away any waste matter that your body has to lose.

▼ Try taking someone's pulse. Do not use your thumb, as that has a pulse of its own. Use a watch to find out the pulse rate.

A breath of fresh air

When you breathe in, you take in air. Oxygen is found in the air. The oxygen goes down into the part of your body you use for breathing, your **lungs**. Inside the lungs there are millions of tiny blood vessels. The blood flowing through the blood vessels picks up the oxygen. Then the blood flows to the heart.

Next, the heart pumps the blood full of oxygen out to the body, through a large blood vessel. This branches out into smaller and smaller tubes. They lead to every part of the body. The blood passes its oxygen from the smallest blood vessels to the tissue that surrounds it.

Stale or used blood, with no oxygen left in it, comes back to the heart. The heart pumps the used blood back to the lungs. There the blood picks up new oxygen and then it is pumped around the body all over again.

The blood carriers

The tubes that carry blood from your heart to the rest of your body are called **arteries**. The blood in arteries is full of oxygen. This makes the blood look bright red. The arteries divide up into smaller and smaller branches. The smallest of all are called **capillaries**. This is where the blood gives up its oxygen, and takes in waste matter. The colour of the blood changes to dark red. The tubes bringing blood back to the heart are called **veins**.

The body beat

You can both hear and feel the beat of your heart as it pumps the blood through your arteries. This beat is called the **pulse**. Put the fingers of one hand on the inside of your other wrist. Find the place just below the bone coming from your thumb. You can feel your pulse beating there. Count the number of beats you feel in a minute. This number is your **pulse rate**.

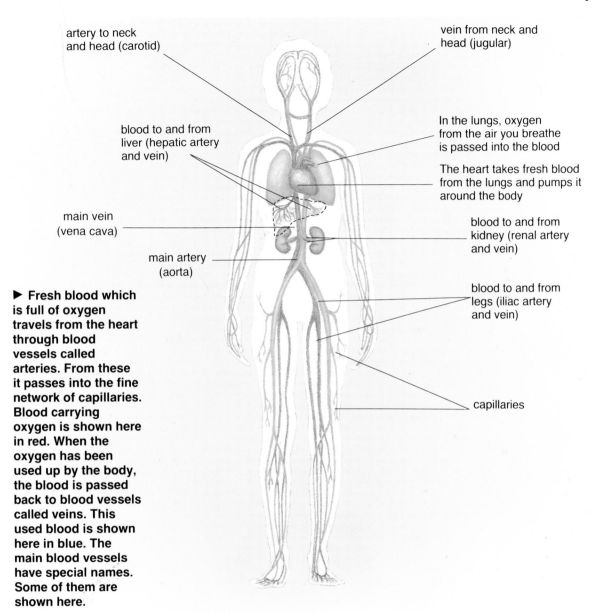

artery to neck
and head (carotid)

vein from neck and
head (jugular)

blood to and from
liver (hepatic artery
and vein)

In the lungs, oxygen
from the air you breathe
is passed into the blood

The heart takes fresh blood
from the lungs and pumps it
around the body

main vein
(vena cava)

blood to and from
kidney (renal artery
and vein)

main artery
(aorta)

blood to and from
legs (iliac artery
and vein)

capillaries

▶ **Fresh blood which
is full of oxygen
travels from the heart
through blood
vessels called
arteries. From these
it passes into the fine
network of capillaries.
Blood carrying
oxygen is shown here
in red. When the
oxygen has been
used up by the body,
the blood is passed
back to blood vessels
called veins. This
used blood is shown
here in blue. The
main blood vessels
have special names.
Some of them are
shown here.**

Did you know?

☆ A normal heart beats about 2500 million times
in an average lifetime.

☆ There are more than 96 000 km of blood
vessels in a human body.

☆ A drop of blood goes round the body more
than 1000 times a day.

☆ It takes just one minute for a drop of blood to
go from your heart, down to your toes and all
the way back again.

☆ Blood leaves the heart travelling at one metre
a second.

☆ A baby has only one litre of blood. A child has
about three litres of blood. An adult has about
five litres of blood.

How the heart works

The heart is a big, powerful **muscle**. It squeezes blood out to the rest of the body, rather like washing-up liquid from a plastic bottle. Heart muscle has to be strong, because it pushes blood along thousands of kilometres of blood vessels all the time.

If you could see the inside of your heart, you would see four different spaces called **chambers**. There are two at the top and two at the bottom. The two at the top are the collecting chambers. They are the left **atrium** and right atrium. The two at the bottom are the pumping chambers. They are called **ventricles**. A wall down the middle divides the heart into two.

Dark red, used blood collects in the top right atrium. When that chamber is full, it passes the blood down into the right ventricle. From there the blood is squeezed and pushed out to the lungs. Here, it loads up with oxygen. The fresh, bright red blood goes back to the heart. It collects in the left atrium. Then the blood is passed down into the bottom left ventricle. The muscle here is thickest and strongest of all. It squeezes hard, sending the blood all round the body.

All this happens in one complete heartbeat. The top chambers squeeze at the same time, passing blood down to the bottom of the heart. A fraction of a second later, the lower chambers also squeeze. They send the blood shooting out to the lungs and all over the body. The blood in the left side of the heart is full of oxygen. The blood in the right side has given up its oxygen. Blood from the two sides does not mix.

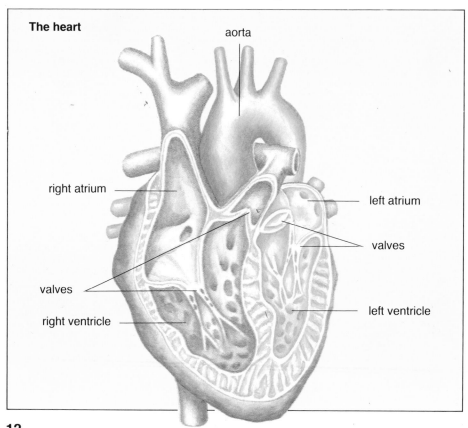

The heart

aorta

right atrium

left atrium

valves

valves

right ventricle

left ventricle

◄ Blood collects in each atrium. From there, it passes down to the ventricle on the same side. The right ventricle sends blood to the lungs. The left ventricle pumps blood from the lungs around the body.

The steady beat

Blood could not travel smoothly through the heart without valves. These are tiny flaps of tissue which only open one way. They stop the blood flowing back the wrong way. When doctors listen to the heartbeat with a stethoscope, they hear a double beat as the heart valves shut tightly.

Inside the heart there is a part which sends out electrical signals. It is a tiny **pacemaker**. These signals tell the heart when to beat. Sometimes the body's own pacemaker does not work properly. This may happen as a person gets old or if they are ill. The pacemaker is no longer able to keep the heart beating at the right rate.

▲ Athletes feel tired and out of breath after a race. Their hearts must beat faster to supply the body with the extra oxygen it needs when it has been working hard.

▼ Here you can see how blood flows in and out of the heart. The movements of blood can take place because there are valves which shut off one part of the heart from another.

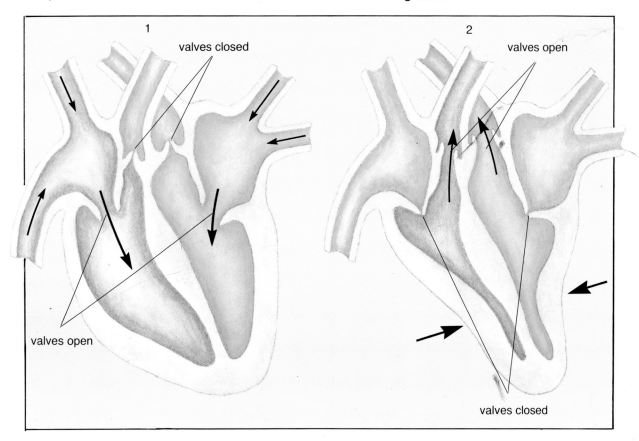

1

valves closed

valves open

2

valves open

valves closed

Blood vessels

There are millions and millions of cells in your body. They are like the bricks a builder uses to build a house. Every single cell needs oxygen and nutrients. Blood carries the oxygen and nutrients to each cell. Blood vessels are the body's transport system. The blood vessels allow blood to go to every cell in the body.

Arteries

Arteries carry blood away from the heart. When the heart squeezes, it pushes blood out into the arteries with great force. The blood is under **pressure**. Arteries have to stand up to this pressure. They have strong, elastic walls. They stretch as the blood surges through them. They spring back again between heartbeats.

▼ These capillaries are carrying blood to the kidneys. A fine network of these tiny tubes carries oxygen-rich blood to cells all over the body.

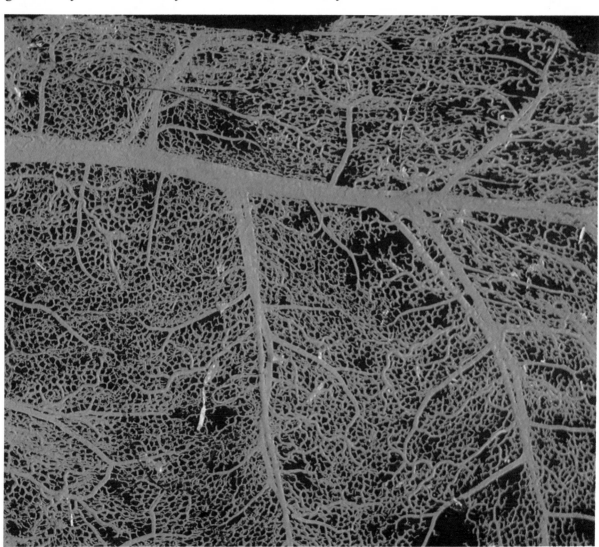

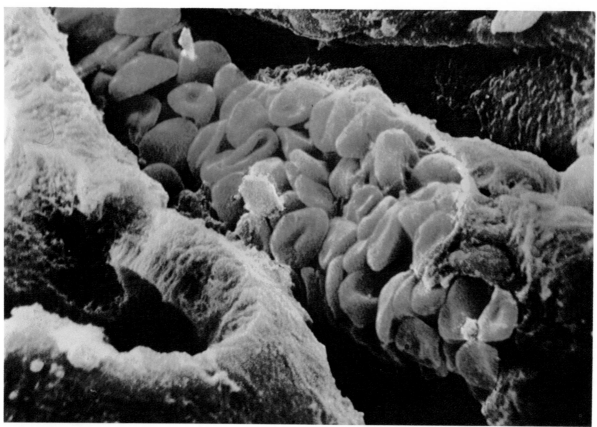

Branching out

The arteries divide up into smaller branches called **arterioles**. The arterioles divide up into even smaller tubes we call capillaries. The capillaries are so tiny that we cannot see them. The walls of capillaries are very thin. They are so thin that oxygen and nutrients can seep through into the cells around them. Waste matter can seep back into the capillaries.

Keeping up the flow

The capillaries join up again into thicker tubes. These are the veins which bring blood back to the heart. The blood in the veins is no longer under pressure. The walls of the veins are not as strong or as elastic as those of the arteries.

Inside the veins, the tiny valves prevent the blood from flowing backwards. This is very useful when blood has to travel uphill.

▲ This photograph was taken with a powerful microscope. It allows us to see the tiny blood cells as they carry oxygen through the capillaries.

There is no push from the heart to keep the blood flowing up the veins. The muscles around the veins do the work. The muscles in your legs and the muscles you use to breathe all help keep the blood flowing.

Control systems in the body check that the right amount of blood is going to the places that need it. If you are sitting awkwardly too little blood may be reaching one of your feet. That foot soon feels cold and prickly. This uncomfortable feeling will make you change position so the blood can reach your foot more easily.

Pressure and pulse

▼ Take your pulse before and after exercise. The pulse rate will be faster afterwards. The faster rate shows how your heart is working hard to rush blood to your muscles.

The push given to the blood by the heart is called **blood pressure**. Each time the heart beats, this wave of pressure flows outwards along the arteries. That wave of pressure, or pulse, is still there as the blood goes up to your head, or down to your feet.

If your heart beats faster, then the pulse is faster too. Find out your normal pulse rate. Now run or skip hard. Check your pulse again. The pulse rate rises because the muscles used in running or skipping need extra food and oxygen. They get this extra food and oxygen from extra blood. The heart has to pump faster to supply them with the extra blood.

The living force

Blood pressure is stronger in arteries than in veins because, the heart is pushing the blood out to the far ends of the body. The artery walls are made up of an elastic material. When it is pushed outwards by blood pressure it squeezes back into shape. This helps push the blood along. Blood pressure forces the blood into the tiny capillaries. By the time the capillaries start to join again, much of the pressure has been used up. This means that the blood pressure in veins is lower than in arteries. The veins are not as elastic as arteries so do not help to maintain the blood pressure.

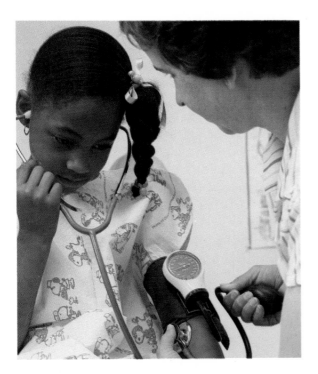

The doctor then takes another measurement. The air in the cuff is let out a little more. This time, the doctor finds the point at which the cuff begins to let the blood through between the heartbeats, as well as during the heartbeats.

A measurement of blood pressure is always given as two numbers, for example $90/60$. The higher number is the pressure when the heart squeezes. The lower number is the pressure between heartbeats.

▲ This girl is having her blood pressure taken. The cuff and pressure gauge can be seen on her arm. The doctor has let the girl listen through the stethoscope.

Taking blood pressure

Doctors check blood pressure because it helps tell them whether a person is healthy or not. To do this, doctors use an inflatable band or cuff that is wrapped around your upper arm. A tube from the cuff leads to a machine that measures pressure. This is called a pressure gauge. The doctor wraps the cuff round the patient's arm and pumps it up. The cuff flattens the artery in the patient's arm and stops blood flowing through it.

The doctor then lets the cuff down just enough for the blood to push its way through when the heart beats. The doctor can tell when the blood is coming through by listening with a stethoscope. The pressure of the blood at this point shows up on the pressure gauge.

▼ Blood keeps going round your body no matter which way up you are. If you stand on your head for long, however, you will begin to feel uncomfortable. You will get red in the face from the build up of blood in your head. When you stand up, you will soon start to feel normal again.

Blood and the lungs

Air comes into the body through the lungs. The lungs are like bellows that suck air in and out. It is vital that they keep working. Without the oxygen from the air that they take in, our body cells would die.

The lungs take up most of the space in your chest. They are protected by the cage of the ribs, and the heart lies between the lungs. A network of thousands of blood vessels runs from the heart to the lungs and back again.

Taking in oxygen

When we breathe in, muscles between the ribs lift the rib cage upwards and outwards. There is another muscle under the lungs. It is a large sheet of muscle called the **diaphragm**. This flattens and pulls downwards. The space in the lungs gets larger. Air rushes in. When we breathe out, the diaphragm relaxes. This lets the lungs get smaller, and air is pushed out.

The inside of the lungs is rather like a sponge. There are masses of tiny holes, called **alveoli**, linked by little tunnels. There are about 750 million alveoli in the human lungs. They are filled with air and covered with blood capillaries. Oxygen from the air seeps into the capillaries. Blood full of oxygen then goes back to the heart.

In the tiny blood vessels inside the lungs, another important change happens. As well as taking in oxygen, the capillaries get rid of a gas called **carbon dioxide**. Carbon dioxide is waste which is made in every single cell. It has to be removed from the body. We get rid of carbon dioxide when we breathe out. Our blood carries carbon dioxide back to the lungs from all over the body.

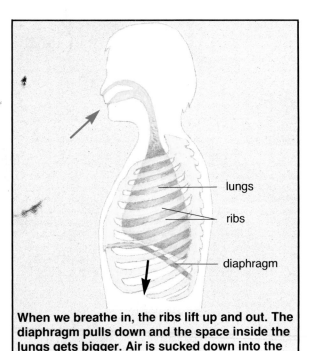

lungs

ribs

diaphragm

When we breathe in, the ribs lift up and out. The diaphragm pulls down and the space inside the lungs gets bigger. Air is sucked down into the space.

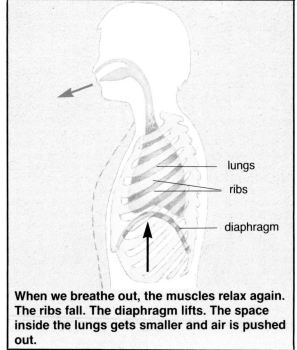

lungs

ribs

diaphragm

When we breathe out, the muscles relax again. The ribs fall. The diaphragm lifts. The space inside the lungs gets smaller and air is pushed out.

The lifeline

We take oxygen into the body and we get rid of carbon dioxide. The oxygen is needed by our body cells. The cells use it in a process called **respiration**. Respiration turns oxygen and food into energy. Energy is the fuel we use for growing, playing, working and staying alive. Blood is the lifeline between the air and every tiny cell in the body.

▶ We need plants, and not just for food. They have tiny oxygen factories in their leaves. They take in our waste carbon dioxide from the air, and give off the oxygen that we need to breathe.

▼ We have two lungs. Each contains millions of alveoli. From these, oxygen passes into the capillaries which are shown here in red. The capillaries shown here in blue pass carbon dioxide from stale blood back into the alveoli.

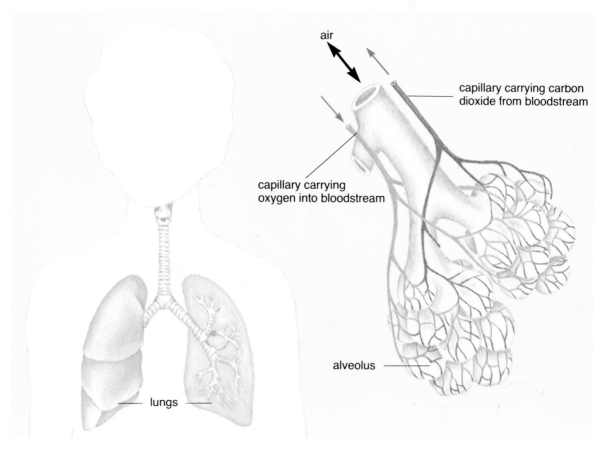

air

capillary carrying carbon dioxide from bloodstream

capillary carrying oxygen into bloodstream

alveolus

lungs

What is blood made of?

▼ Doctors can look at blood cells through a microscope. They can count the different kinds of cell, and check their size and shape. More white blood cells than normal could mean that the blood is working hard to fight off a disease.

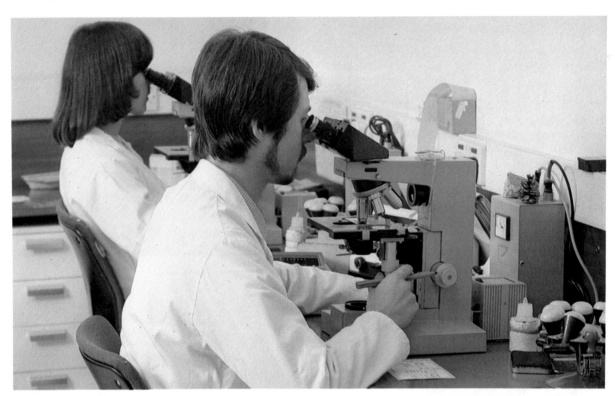

Blood is made up of different kinds of cells. Each type of blood cell has a different job to do. The cells travel around the body in a watery yellowish liquid called **plasma**. Plasma also has food parts, waste, salts and other materials floating in it. Blood cells are made mainly in the tissue called **bone marrow**. Bone marrow is found in the middle of the large bones in your body.

Oxygen rafts

The most common kind of blood cells are the **red blood cells**. There are five million or more in a single pin-prick of blood. Bone marrow is busy making more all the time. It is the red blood cells that give blood its colour. The cells contain a red colouring called **haemoglobin**.

Haemoglobin is important because it carries oxygen and carbon dioxide. Red blood cells are like tiny rafts. They load up with oxygen in the lungs. On their journey around the body they unload the oxygen. Then they take carbon dioxide on board instead, and flow back again to the lungs.

Another type of blood cell is the **white blood cell**. There are not nearly as many white blood cells as red ones. There are just one or two white cells for every thousand red cells. White cells are larger than red cells, and they can change their shape. Their job is to protect us from illness.

In the air around us, there are millions of very tiny creatures which can make us ill. These **germs** carry minor illnesses such as the common cold, as well as much more serious diseases. If we become ill, we usually get better before long. This is because white cells act as an army in our bodies which attacks and destroys germs. White cells can grow in number very quickly. Some can change shape to surround the germs and 'eat' them.

Sticking together

If you cut your finger, the first thing that happens is that blood oozes out. If the wound is a serious one, blood may pour out. Before long the blood flow slows down and stops. This is because of **platelets**. Platelets in the blood are smaller than other blood cells. In a sample of blood that had 1000 blood cells you would find about 200 platelets.

When you cut yourself and bleed, the body has to defend itself. The platelets become sticky and cling together. They slow down the blood flow. Then they join up and form a crust to protect the wound. This is called a scab.

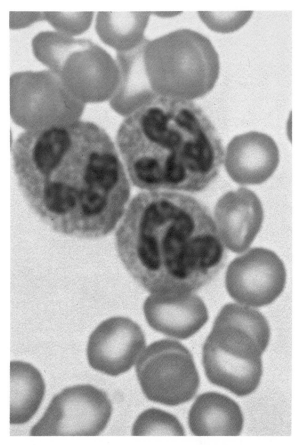

▲ The large cells in this picture are white blood cells. They are much bigger than the red cells round about. White cells defend the body against germs.

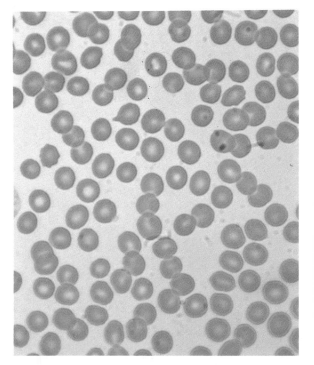

◀ Red blood cells are like round cushions which are thicker at the edges than they are in the middle. Capillaries are so small that the red cells have to squeeze through in single file. This is when they release their oxygen.

Did you know?
☆ Red blood cells are made at a rate of 90 to 100 million a minute.
☆ Red blood cells live for about 4 months.
☆ White blood cells live for about 7 to 14 days.
☆ Platelets live for about 8 to 10 days.
☆ One red blood cell makes 170 000 journeys round the body in its lifetime.
☆ In every drop of blood there are 250 million red blood cells, 400 000 white blood cells and 15 million platelets.

Fighting disease

There are two main kinds of germ. The first is **bacteria**, which are found in many places. Many bacteria are useful. They help break down many waste materials such as the waste matter of the body. Some bacteria cause illnesses. **Viruses** are even smaller than bacteria. We know less about how they work. Viruses can only make you ill when they get inside your body cells.

When harmful bacteria or viruses get into our bodies, white blood cells rush to attack them. If the white cells cannot destroy the germs straight away they make their own kind of poison for that particular germ. This poison is called an **antibody**.

Safe from attack

When certain germs get into your body, your white cells start to make antibodies against them. This takes a little while and you might feel ill for a few days. Once the antibodies are in your blood, they are there forever.

Doctors can trick the body into making antibodies against some illnesses. They inject a dose of very weak or dead germs into the patient. This is called a **vaccination**. One of the illnesses which can be prevented by vaccination is measles. The virus given by the vaccination is not strong enough to give you the illness. The body is tricked into making antibodies to measles. The next time a really powerful measles virus tries to attack you, the antibody is ready and waiting. The measle germs are killed off at once. You are now **immune** to measles.

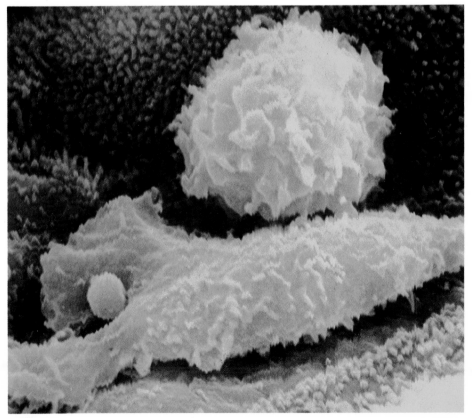

◄ The small round object is an attacking germ. A white blood cell surrounds and swallows the germ. It destroys the germ, leaving only some waste matter. Waste like this drains into the lymphatic system.

► Most children have vaccinations quite often, from the time they are babies onwards. The injection is over quickly and does not hurt much. Catching the disease would be much worse!

Cleaning the blood

A clear, watery liquid called **lymph** also flows through our bodies. To do this it uses a network known as the **lymphatic system**. All along the system there are bean-sized **lymph nodes**. A group of these nodes makes up a **gland**.

There are extra white blood cells in the lymph nodes. The body uses the extra white cells in the lymphatic system to help it attack germs that have entered the body. When you are ill, you may have painful swollen glands in your neck, armpits, and at the top of your legs. The swelling is the result of the battle going on between the germs and the white blood cells.

◄ Waste and extra fluid from the bloodstream are collected in the system of lymph vessels. These go all over the body. They clean the lymph and return it to the bloodstream near the heart.

The lymphatic system

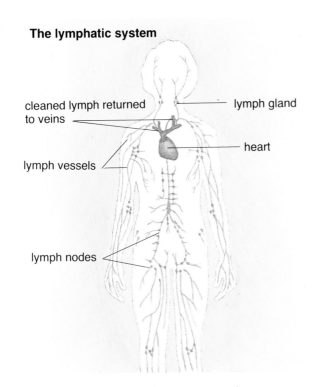

cleaned lymph returned to veins

lymph gland

heart

lymph vessels

lymph nodes

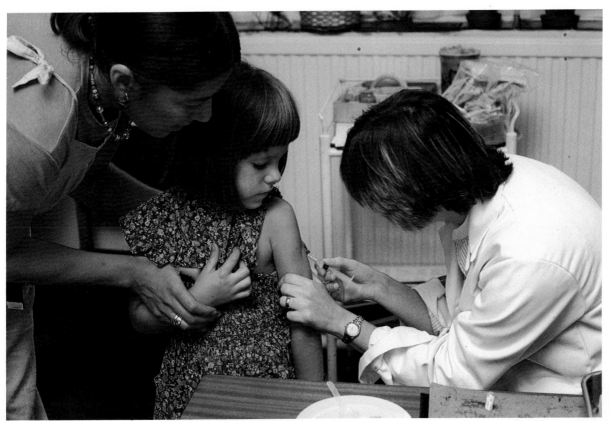

Fuel and waste

A car needs petrol to make it go. Our bodies need food for the same reason. The transport system that takes food round the body is the blood.

Breakfast cereal, milk, bread and everything else you eat has to be broken down into very tiny bits. The bits have to be small enough to get into your blood. This process is called **digestion**. It starts as soon as you start to chew your food. In your body there are substances which work with other things to make changes. These substances are called **chemicals**.

In your stomach, chemicals called digestive juices mix in with the food. They work on the food breaking it down still further. The food then passes into a long tube called the **small intestine**.

The digestive system

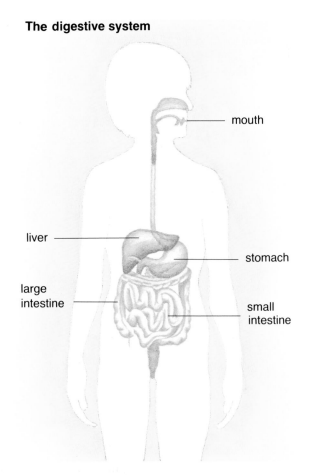

▲ The food we eat is broken up into tiny bits by our digestive systems. The useful parts are passed into the bloodstream. This carries the nutrients to every cell in our bodies.

▼ The inside of the small intestine is covered in villi. Nutrients pass through the villi into the blood. This blood then flows to the liver.

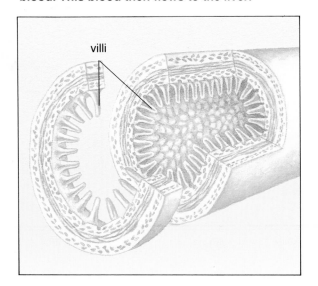

The inside walls of the small intestine are covered with tiny fingerlike **villi**. They give the intestine a very large surface area. If you spread it out flat it would cover a whole tennis court. The villi contain many millions of blood capillaries. The nutrients from the food seep through the walls of the villi into the blood. The blood then travels all over your body to carry nutrients to the cells.

The remains of food pass to the **large intestine** where they are processed further. You get rid of the waste when you go to the lavatory.

The blood filter

Low down in the middle of your back are two important organs, your **kidneys**. Every day, your blood flows through the kidneys hundreds of times. The water in the blood is squeezed out and filtered. Unwanted waste matter and poisons are removed. The main waste is **urea**. This is made when food is digested. Too much urea in the blood is poisonous.

Most of the water is put back into the bloodstream. Any water that the body does not need drains away into the **bladder**. The wastes and poisons are dissolved in the waste water. When the bladder starts to fill up, we feel the need to go to the lavatory. This gets rid of the wastes filtered from the blood.

If the kidneys do not work properly, doctors use a kidney machine to take waste matter from the blood. One kidney is only as big as a fist. A kidney machine is as big as a cupboard and does not work as well as a real kidney.

More than half of our blood is made of water. The kidneys contain many tiny filters. The water passes through the filters and is cleaned. Most of the water goes back into the bloodstream again.

The food processor

The largest organ in the body is the **liver**. This has many different jobs to do. Blood flows from the intestines loaded with food. The first place it goes to is the liver. The liver stores much of this food. It can be sent out later to wherever it is needed.

Used red blood cells also end up in the liver. Any useful parts of them are stored, to be reused later.

How water is passed from the body

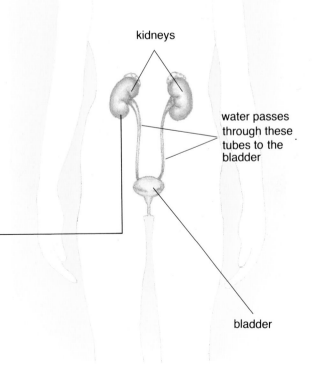

kidneys

water passes through these tubes to the bladder

bladder

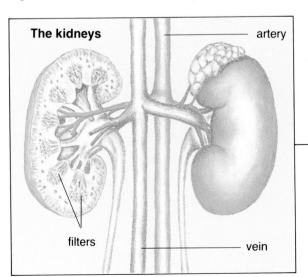

The kidneys

artery

filters

vein

A warm body

Some animals rely on the Sun to keep them warm. When it gets cold their bodies slow down almost to a standstill. They are **cold-blooded**. Humans are **warm-blooded**. We make our own heat so that our bodies stay within a degree or two of the same temperature. This is useful because it means we can stay active whether it is freezing cold or blazing hot weather.

Central heating

When fuel burns on a fire or in a car, it makes heat. The same is true of the fuel our bodies take in. Most of the food we eat is used to make heat. Blood acts like the water in the pipes in a central heating system. Blood carries the heat and spreads it all over the body.

At the heart of the system is the liver, which acts as the central heating boiler. The liver is helped by muscles. That is why we feel hot after running a race. The active muscles burn up extra food from the liver. When they use that food, it makes extra heat.

The muscles may sometimes have been so active that we feel too hot. Blood also helps to cool us down. Tiny blood vessels near the skin get larger or **dilate**. We start to look red in the face. More blood comes to the surface of our bodies and heat is given off into the air.

If we get too cold, blood vessels near the skin shut down. This stops heat escaping

◄ This lizard is cold-blooded. This means that its body cannot make its own heat. When lizards are cold, they can only move slowly. They therefore lie in the Sun and soak up the heat like sun-bathers. Humans are warm-blooded. Our bodies can make heat to keep us warm.

through the skin. It makes the skin look pale and even slightly blue. Shivering also helps. Tiny jerks by the muscles under the skin make the muscles work harder. This helps make extra heat to warm us up.

▶ Strip thermometers are useful for taking the temperatures of young children. They are placed on the forehead and kept there for one minute. N is for normal. Mercury thermometers are usually placed under the tongue for a minute or two.

▼ After a hard workout, people feel hot. They sometimes sweat and their faces become red. This is because their muscles have been working hard. They have given off a lot of extra heat. Blood vessels fill up near the skin's surface. They give off heat through the skin and help to cool down the body.

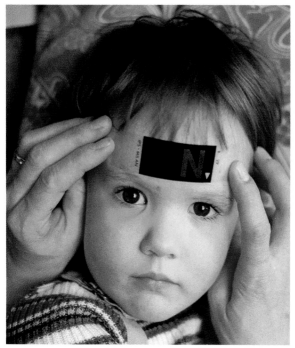

Taking temperatures

The normal temperature of the body is about 37°C. This often goes up when you are ill. A higher temperature can mean that the body is fighting off an attack by germs. Viruses seem to like the body's normal temperature. When the temperature rises, it is more difficult for the viruses to grow. Unfortunately, a high temperature makes you feel tired and uncomfortable. Medicines can help bring body temperature down, so that you feel better.

Temperature is measured by using a **thermometer**. Body temperature is higher inside our bodies than on the surface of the skin. A mercury thermometer has mercury in it that expands as it warms up. The mercury moves along a narrow tube. The tube is marked off in degrees, showing different temperature levels. There is another kind of thermometer called a strip thermometer. This has tiny pieces of a special material in it which change colour as they get warmer. A number or letter shows the correct temperature.

Body control

Our bodies have their own patterns of activity and rest. Meals, work, playtime and sleep all follow in the same order day by day. Chemicals called **hormones** play a large part in making the different parts of our bodies do the right thing at the right time. Some hormones are made in the **endocrine glands**. These glands are found near blood vessels. The glands pour their hormones straight into the bloodstream.

The chemical messengers

Hormones control how fast we grow, and when and how quickly we digest food. They also control how much water we keep in our bodies and our heart rate. Hormones tell certain cells to start working and others to stop or to go more slowly. Hormones may wash over every cell in the body, but each hormone has its own special target. It will cause change in certain cells, but other cells will not be affected by it.

Body changes

You can probably remember the feeling you get just before taking a test, or before the start of a race you really want to win. You might have a feeling like butterflies in your tummy. Your heart starts to thump in your chest. You breathe more deeply. All these things happen because of a hormone called **adrenalin**.

▶ The blood carries hormones which control the way in which our bodies develop. Some hormones are passed into the bloodstream by endocrine glands. Other glands by-pass the bloodstream and make the hormone act directly on a part of the body.

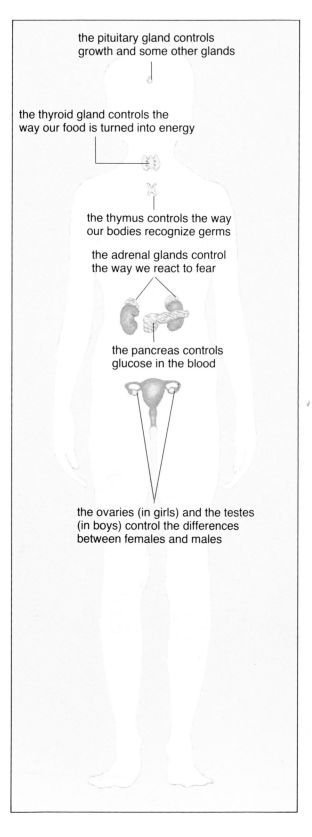

the pituitary gland controls growth and some other glands

the thyroid gland controls the way our food is turned into energy

the thymus controls the way our bodies recognize germs

the adrenal glands control the way we react to fear

the pancreas controls glucose in the blood

the ovaries (in girls) and the testes (in boys) control the differences between females and males

Adrenalin acts on many parts of the body. It gets the body ready to run very fast or try very hard to do something. Before you even start to run a race, your heart is beating faster. It pumps extra nutrients and oxygen to your leg muscles so that they are ready to work hard the moment you need them.

The hormone that controls the rate at which we grow is made in the **pituitary** gland, which is just below the front of the brain. It is very important that we have enough of this hormone.

▼ A racing car waits for the start of a race. The driver feels tense and excited. The hormone adrenalin is working in his body. Adrenalin gives our bodies an extra surge of power when we are scared.

▲ We go on growing for about the first twenty years of our lives. The hormone that controls growth is made in the pituitary gland. People without enough growth hormone do not grow as fast as they should. They will be shorter than normal. Too much growth hormone means that they will grow taller than normal.

The right balance

Many different hormones flow round the body. There has to be just the right amount of each hormone to keep the body working properly.

One example is the hormone **thyroxin**. This is made in the **thyroid gland** which is in the neck. Thyroxin controls how fast we burn up food. People with too much thyroxin use up their food too quickly. They will be rather thin and their heart rate will be faster than normal. If people's bodies do not make enough thyroxin, they will be fat and slow-moving. Too much or too little thyroxin makes people ill.

Healing

A cut or graze breaks the skin and the blood vessels under the skin. This allows blood to leave the body. Blood is precious so the body quickly takes action to stop the bleeding.

First the platelets start to stick together. The blood gets thick and jelly-like. It forms a plug or **clot** which seals the hole.

This alone may be enough to stop the bleeding. At the same time, the blood vessels get narrower. This cuts down the amount of blood flowing to the cut. Less blood can leak away.

Next, a scab forms. Chemicals in the blood near the clot make thin strands of a substance called **fibrin**. The fibrin grows into a cobweb-like net which traps more platelets and blood cells in it. Gradually a solid scab builds up. It prevents dirt and germs getting in the body. Meanwhile, the cells under the scab start to repair the damage.

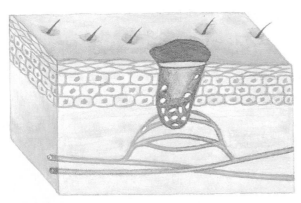

▲ Dirt and germs can get into a cut very easily. Blood flowing from the cut washes some of the germs away. White cells come to the wound and swallow up the remaining germs.

▲ When you cut yourself, platelets in your blood stick together. Strands of fibrin trap the platelets, forming a seal over the cut. This stops the bleeding.

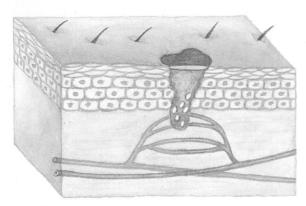

▲ New skin tissue starts to grow in order to repair the damage done by the wound. If the cut has been very bad, the new tissue may not grow back in the same way. It may leave a scar.

▲ When the skin is nearly healed, the scab falls away. Scabs should not be picked before they are ready to fall away. New cells may be damaged and germs may be let in.

Cleaning up

The surface of your skin looks clean. In fact, it is covered with millions of bacteria. A cut lets in dirt and germs. The body has to get rid of them as quickly as possible. White cells rush to the damaged area to swallow up the dirt and germs. You sometimes see a yellowish liquid round a bad cut. This is **pus** which is made up of dead white cells and the rubbish they have cleared up.

In just a few hours, a hard scab forms. Over the next few days, new skin grows under it. Once the skin has healed, the scab shrinks and drops off.

Bumps and bruises

A bump or knock often leaves a swollen, sore place. Later, a bruise appears. The bruise means that blood vessels under the skin have been damaged. Blood cells leak into the tissue under the skin. In a few days, white cells eat up these blood cells. The bruise is often coloured blue, purple or black. It fades to yellow before it disappears.

The area around a cut or bruise is often swollen. The swelling is painful but it is part of the body's repair programme. Blood vessels near the cut or bruise expand and leak. More blood can flow into the area to help it heal. Plasma and white cells seep into the nearby tissue.

▼ If you looked at a wound through a microscope, you could see the network of fibrin trapping the blood cells. This makes the blood clot. In this picture the red blood cells have been shown in yellow so that they can be seen more easily.

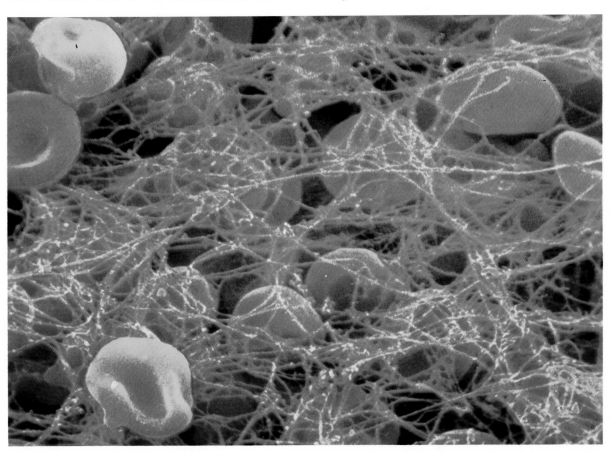

Blood types

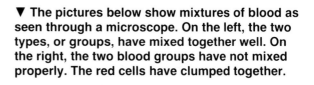

▼ The pictures below show mixtures of blood as seen through a microscope. On the left, the two types, or groups, have mixed together well. On the right, the two blood groups have not mixed properly. The red cells have clumped together.

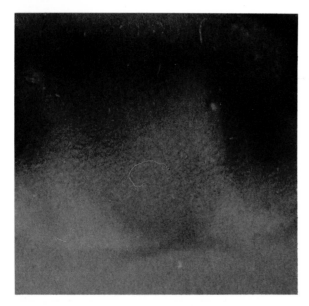

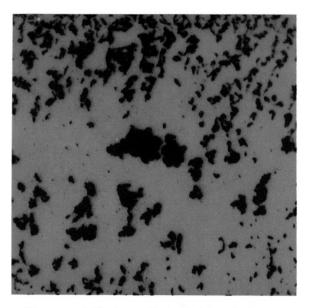

All blood looks the same under a microscope, but there are some important differences. There are some substances that cause the body to make antibodies. These are called **antigens**. Antigens are carried in red blood cells. However, the antigens in the blood of one person are not always of the same type as those in someone else.

Four groups of blood

In 1900, an Austrian scientist called Karl Landsteiner worked out that there are four main types, or groups, of blood. He found out how the antigens in one blood group react with all the other groups. He called the groups A, B, AB, and O.

Blood in group A contains A antigens. It will make antibodies against B antigens. Group B contains B antigens. It will make antibodies against A antigens. So if blood group A is given to someone with B blood, the B blood makes antibodies against the A blood. The antibodies from group B blood

will try to kill the cells in A blood. A person can get very sick if this happens and might even die. Group O blood can be given safely to people with A, B or AB blood. However, group O people can only be given type O blood. Blood groups that can mix safely are said to be **compatible**.

In 1940, scientists carried out tests with Rhesus monkeys and found a number of substances. One of these, called **Rhesus factor**, or Rh-factor, was found in the red blood cells of 85 per cent of all people. These people have Rhesus positive blood. The other 15 per cent have Rhesus negative blood.

If you are Rhesus positive and your blood is given to someone who is Rhesus negative, that person's blood would make antibodies to your blood. Those antibodies would stay in the other person's blood. If, later on, more Rhesus positive blood were given, the blood antibodies would destroy the red cells in the new blood.

Testing and matching

Blood has to be carefully matched to make sure it will mix safely. The most common groups of blood are A, B and O groups which are Rhesus positive. There are many more sub-groups as well, although they are much rarer. Scientists make careful tests and keep computer records. They can match people with rare blood groups who live thousands of kilometres apart.

▶ People from the same part of the world often have the same blood type, or group. South American Indians, such as this family from Peru, often belong to blood group O. The Inca people, who once lived in Peru, learned how to give blood transfusions hundreds of years ago. The operation was often successful because most Incas belonged to the same blood group.

▼ The victim of an accident is rushed to hospital in an ambulance. If a patient is losing blood, doctors must find out quickly to which group it belongs.

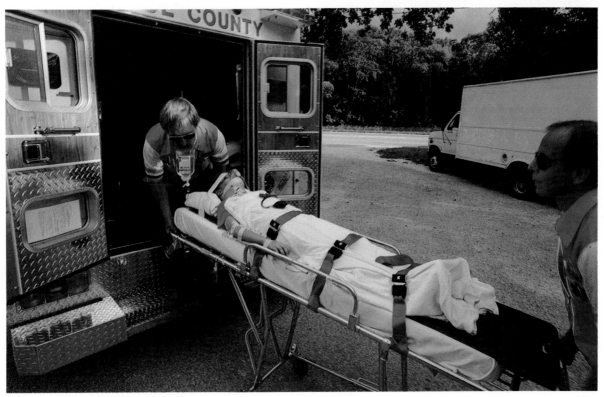

New blood for old

A person who has a bad accident might lose a lot of blood. If an artery is cut, blood spurts out under pressure from the heart. The lost blood has to be replaced quickly.

Blood from a healthy person is put into the veins of the accident victim. Doctors do this by giving a blood transfusion. People who have serious operations or something wrong with their own blood may also need transfusions of healthy blood. It is only during the last 40 years that doctors have been able to do blood transfusions safely. They are now widely used and save millions of lives.

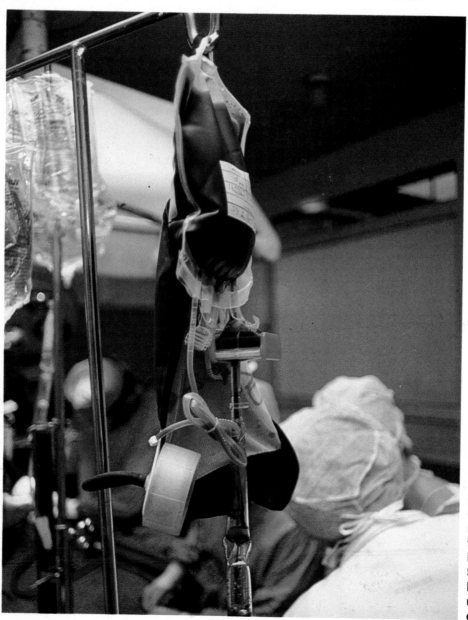

◄ A supply of new blood is given to a patient who is losing blood during an operation. The new blood will have been carefully checked to make sure that it is of the right type and that it is free from germs. Sometimes many litres of blood are used during an operation.

Giving blood

Healthy adults can give small amounts of their own blood without any harm to themselves. Someone who gives blood is called a **donor**. A donor can give about 0.5 litres of blood at a time without any problems. The body makes up the lost plasma in less than one day. It takes between two and six weeks to replace the lost red cells.

When a donor gives blood, a needle is put into a vein in the arm. It hurts no more than a pinprick. The blood flows along a thin tube into a container. This has chemicals in it which keep the blood from clotting. It also has special food in it to keep the living cells alive.

The blood is then tested to find its group and to make sure it is not carrying any disease. It is labelled and stored in a **blood bank** at 4°C. At this temperature it lasts for up to a month. After this, only the plasma can still be used.

Often blood is separated out into its parts, that is plasma, cells and platelets. This is because a patient may only need part of the blood. It would be wasteful to give the whole blood. For example, a patient may not have enough of his own platelets. The doctor will give him a transfusion containing just the plasma and platelets. The red and white cells can be used for another patient.

▲ Blood that has been taken from donors is stored in a blood bank. It must be ready for use at any time. Each container is labelled with details of the blood.

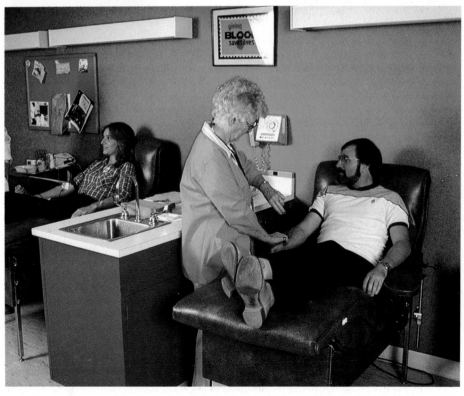

▶ Hospitals are always in need of supplies of healthy blood from donors. Giving blood can help save lives, and it does not harm the donor in any way.

Illnesses

Most hearts work very well for years and years. However, sometimes things may go wrong with the heart and blood circulation.

Sometimes, when a baby is born, the heart is not formed correctly, and cannot pump properly. Surgeons have to operate.

As we get older, we may have trouble because of the way we live. For example, eating too much fat leads to fatty lumps in the arteries. The heart has to pump harder to push blood through the half-blocked blood vessels.

Like the rest of the body, the heart itself needs blood that is rich in oxygen. The arteries going to the heart are the **coronary arteries**. If they get blocked, blood going to the heart is cut off. A **heart attack** follows. It is very painful and the heart itself may stop beating. With quick treatment, the heart can often be restarted. Many people who have had heart attacks get better, but they must take care of themselves.

▼ If we eat too much fatty food, our arteries become blocked. You can see what has happened in this picture. The blockage strains the heart and makes us ill.

Narrowed arteries

fatty deposits

blood

artery

▲ Modern medical treatment has made it possible for people suffering from haemophilia to lead active lives, although they must always be careful of wounding themselves. These youngsters are on a rock-climbing expedition in Wales.

Problems with your blood

Sometimes things go wrong with the blood. If someone feels tired all the time and has no energy, they may have something wrong with their red blood cells. Not enough oxygen is being carried round the body. This is called **anaemia**. It is caused when the body does not get enough **iron**. Iron is needed to make healthy red cells. Extra iron in tablets, or in the right kind of food, usually cures the anaemia.

Some boys are born with blood that does not clot properly. This condition is called **haemophilia**. For people with haemophilia even a tiny cut could be dangerous because it is so difficult to stop the bleeding. Before blood transfusions were widely used, these people could not lead normal, active lives. Now they can have transfusions of plasma and platelets. This means that their blood will be able to clot if they cut themselves.

Making
people better

▼ Doctors can use an ECG to find out if the patient's heart is beating as it should. Electrical signals from the heart show up on the screen. Having an ECG test does not hurt.

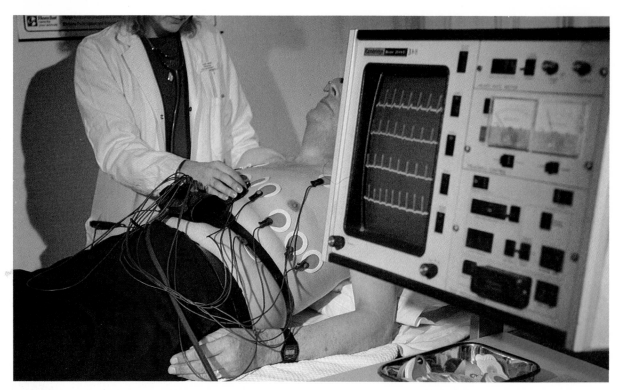

When someone feels ill, they can go to their doctor for advice. The doctor can tell a lot about illness by asking questions. Patients can say if they have a pain, or feel tired, or out of breath. Simple tools like a stethoscope and blood pressure gauge help the doctor to make further checks. The patient may have to be sent to hospital.

There are many machines in hospitals to help the doctor decide what is wrong. The patient's heartbeat can be recorded on an **electrocardiograph**, or ECG for short. The normal heart beats at a regular rate. Each time it beats, it sends out an electrical signal. Special pads are put on the patient's body. They pick up the electrical signals from the heart. The ECG machine turns the signal into a wavy line which it draws

out on a long roll paper. When the doctors look at this, they can see how the pattern made by the line differs from the pattern made by a normal heart. It helps them decide which part of the heart is not working properly.

Heart surgery

Today, heart surgeons can put right all kinds of faults in the heart. Some babies are born with a 'hole in the heart'. This is a break in the wall down the middle of the heart. The 'hole' allows used blood to leak through into blood that has fresh oxygen. The pressure in the heart is wrong and it cannot pump properly. Forty years ago, many of these children died. Today, surgeons operate to seal up the hole.

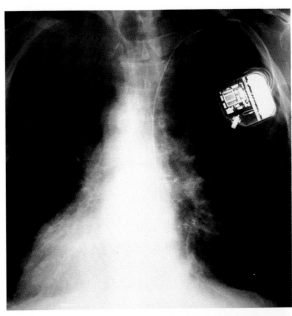

New parts

As we get older, we may suffer from arteries that become clogged by fat. The arteries going to the heart itself may even suffer. Surgeons can now take a blood vessel from a place that is not clogged, such as the leg, and transfer it to the heart. Artificial parts, such as a valve or pacemaker can also be put in the heart to make it work better.

It is even possible to take out a faulty heart and put in a healthy one. The problem with such **heart transplants** is that the body does not like tissue that is not its own. It tries to destroy the new tissue. Doctors have to use powerful drugs to stop this happening.

▲ This X-ray picture shows the inside of a patient's chest. On the right you can see an artificial pacemaker for the heart. It has been put in during an operation.

▶ Samples are prepared for the microscope in a laboratory. Doctors take a sample of patients' blood in order to find out if they are suffering from any disease.

First aid

When there is an accident, you can sometimes help someone before a doctor or an ambulance arrives. First aid can stop injuries getting worse. It can sometimes save lives. An accident can be rather frightening, even if you are not hurt yourself. To give good first aid, you have to stay calm and know exactly the right thing to do.

There are many societies, such as the Red Cross, that run first aid courses. You can find the telephone number of a branch near you in the phone book or by asking at your local library. Everyone should know the basics of first aid. You never know when you might be able to help.

▲ Someone with a heart attack has pain in the chest and maybe in the arms. They may collapse. You must get help straight away. If there is no one nearby who can help, telephone the Emergency Services and explain what has happened.

▲ When a person faints, they usually recover after a minute or two. Get them to sit with their head between their knees. This gets the blood back to the brain and stops the feeling of faintness. If you are in a hot, stuffy place, open windows and doors to let in fresh air.

▲ The blood vessels in your nose are delicate. A bump or even a change in the weather will often break a blood vessel, and make your nose bleed.
1 Pinch your nose gently to stop the blood running out. This gives the blood a chance to clot.
2 Do not tip your head back or the blood will go down the back of your throat.
3 Do not blow your nose for about half an hour after the bleeding stops.

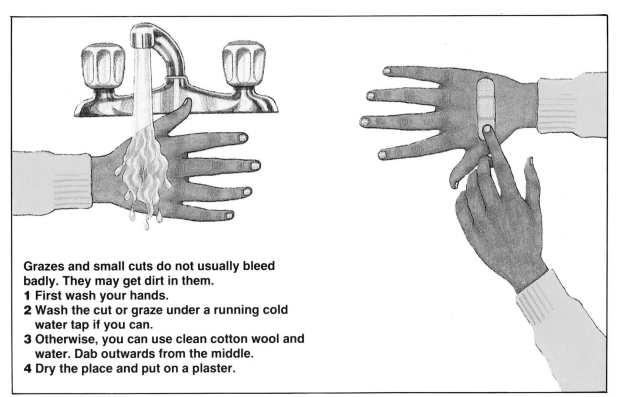

Grazes and small cuts do not usually bleed
badly. They may get dirt in them.
1 First wash your hands.
2 Wash the cut or graze under a running cold
   water tap if you can.
3 Otherwise, you can use clean cotton wool and
   water. Dab outwards from the middle.
4 Dry the place and put on a plaster.

If blood is spurting out from a cut, it is serious.
Get help from an adult straight away. If there is
no one else around, use a clean hankerchief.
Any piece of rolled-up cloth will do in an
emergency. Press it down hard on the wound.
Keep your hand there until someone comes.

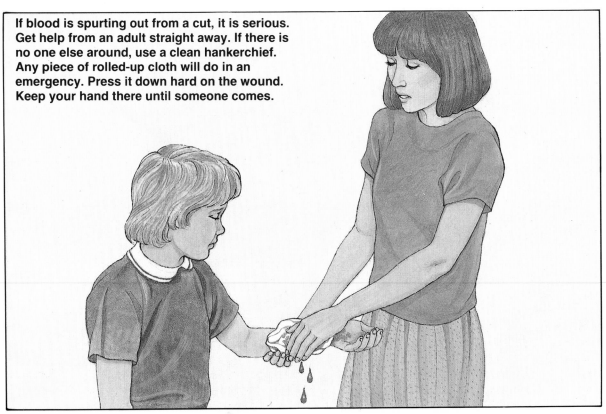

Health and your heart

Your body separates your food into nutrients. Different nutrients are used by the body in a different way. Too much or too little of a particular nutrient may be bad for you.

We know that many people get heart disease in the United States and many countries in Europe. It is much less common in the countries of Africa and Asia. The main reason is that the people of these countries eat a very different kind of diet. In countries where there is more heart disease the people eat much more fat and sugar, and less fruit and vegetables. This tends to make them fat, and it is bad for the heart. In Europe, even some very young children have been found to have the first signs of blocked or narrowed arteries because their diet contains too much fat.

The worst kinds of fat we eat contain a substance called **cholesterol**. Most animal fats are high in cholesterol. Most vegetable fats contain very little. People should make sure they do not eat too much fatty meat, butter, cheese and eggs. They should use vegetable-based magarine, low-fat cheese and food cooked in vegetable oil.

The heart and blood need all kinds of nutrients to stay healthy. The blood needs iron to make red cells. Iron is found in liver and green vegetables. The blood needs small amounts of **vitamins**. Vitamins are found in many foods, but especially in fresh fruit and vegetables.

Smoking

Tobacco smoke contains many different chemicals. They cover the lungs in black tar. Smokers often feel short of breath because oxygen cannot get into the blood as easily as it should.

Smokers get more chest infections. The smoke can even make their arteries get blocked up more quickly. Smoking is very bad for your health.

◄ **Our blood needs a supply of oxygen from the lungs. If we fill our lungs with cigarette smoke, instead, we damage our health. Smoking can kill you.**

▲ The skins or husks of foods like fruit, vegetables, rice and wheat contain many vital nutrients. Sometimes, when these foods are peeled, or cooked for too long, these nutrients can be lost.

▼ Doughnuts, cakes and sugary drinks contain a lot of sugar and fats. Food that has been made up in factories, even vegetables, often has extra sugar in it. A healthy diet should include a variety of fresh foods.

Staying healthy

If your muscles are not used they get weaker and weaker. If you look at a dancer or a sportsman, you will see that their muscles are firm and round. Someone who never does any exercise has weak, flabby muscles.

The heart is a muscle like any other muscle in the body. The more it is used the stronger it gets. The kind of exercise that makes your heart work is in activities like running, skipping and swimming. They all go on for quite a long time and they make you get out of breath. Your lungs work harder and your heart has to pump more strongly to send the blood round to other working muscles.

▲ A weightlifter has huge muscles but he may not be as fit as a runner. Short bursts of exercise are not as good for the heart as longer-lasting exercise.

◄ Yoga is a kind of exercise which helps keep people supple and healthy. They also learn to breathe deeply. This brings oxygen into the bloodstream.

▲ Exercise is good for everyone. It makes you feel fitter and more lively. It also keeps you healthy over a long period of time. Heart disease can start in young children. Exercise and the right kind of food will help you keep fit and healthy all your life.

When you try out a new sport, you may feel tired after the first time. Next time you try it, it is not so bad. Your muscles, including the heart, get stronger. This is why athletes go into training. Each training session builds up the heart and lungs a little more. Gradually, the athlete gets fitter.

The kind of exercise that works the heart and lungs is called **aerobic**. It simply means 'with oxygen'. Short, sharp bursts of exercise are not as good for the heart as aerobic exercise which goes on for some time. Exercise like weight-lifting or short

sprinting is over and done with before the heart really begins to work hard. That kind of exercise is called **anaerobic**, which means 'without oxygen'.

More people have cars than ever before. More people sit down and watch television than ever. One reason why heart disease is increasing is that many people do not get enough exercise.

A healthy life

Most people do not know that there is anything wrong with their heart and blood circulation until it is too late to do anything about it. Eating the right things and taking exercise is not difficult. Lots of the food that is good for you tastes nice too. You do not have to go to a special class to exercise. Riding your bicycle, swimming, skipping or playing football are all fun. It is nice to know that they are good for your heart too.

Glossary

adrenalin: a substance in the body that helps the body react quickly. Adrenalin increases the amount of blood going to the heart, muscles and brain

aerobic: with oxygen. Aerobic exercise makes you use up oxygen more quickly than usual

alveoli: the tiny pockets full of air which make up your lungs

anaemia: a blood disease. The body cannot make enough red colouring or red parts in the blood. This makes people feel tired and weak

anaerobic: without oxygen. Anaerobic exercise does not make you use up oxygen more quickly than usual

antibody: a substance made by your body which protects the body against illness

antigen: a substance in the blood that makes it produce antibodies to protect the body

arteriole: one of the small tubes through which the blood flows away from the heart. Arterioles are joined to larger and smaller tubes

artery: one of the main tubes that carry fresh blood from your heart, out to parts of your body

atrium: one of the two small chambers at the top of your heart

bacteria: tiny creatures that can only be seen with a strong microscope. Some are harmful and cause disease. Others are useful and eat up dead plants and animals

bladder: the bag-like part of the body where waste liquid, or urine, collects. You empty your bladder when you go to the lavatory

blood: a red liquid found inside the body. It carries food, oxygen and other important things to every part of the body

blood bank: a place where blood is stored after it has been collected

blood-letting: making a sick person bleed to help them get well. Blood-letting was widely used before doctors understood how the body works

blood pressure: the amount of force used to push blood along the tubes away from the heart. It can be measured at two points. One is when the heart is squeezing, the other when the heart is relaxed

blood vessel: any tube which carries the blood around inside your body

bone marrow: the substance inside bones where blood is made

capillary: one of a network of tiny tubes which carry blood to and from every part of the body

carbon dioxide: a gas made up of carbon and oxygen. We get rid of it as waste when we breathe out

cell: a very small part or unit. Most living things are made up of millions of cells

chamber: an enclosed space. The heart has four chambers

cholesterol: a fatty substance carried in the blood

chemical: any substance which can change when joined or mixed with another substance

circulation: a movement around in a certain space. Blood circulates around the body

clot: the joining together of parts of a liquid so that it stops flowing. When you cut yourself, the blood quickly clots and stops the bleeding

cold-blooded: describing an animal which cannot control its own body temperature

compatible: to go with or fit with something else, such as when one substance mixes well with another

coronary arteries: the tubes that supply blood to the heart so that it can keep working

diaphragm: a large muscle in the body that separates the chest from the stomach and makes the lungs work

digestion: the way food is broken down so that it can be used by the body

dilate: to get larger or wider. When blood vessels dilate they allow more blood to flow through them

dissect: to cut up something carefully to find out how it is made and how the parts fit together

donor: someone who gives something to somebody else. A blood donor gives some of their blood to someone who needs it

electrocardiograph: a machine which draws out a graph of a person's heartbeat. It is known as an ECG for short

endocrine gland: a group of cells which make substances which affect other cells

fibrin: a substance in the blood that helps the blood to thicken so that it cannot flow out of a cut

germ: a tiny living thing than can cause diseases. Germs can only be seen with a very strong microscope

gland: a part of the body which makes a substance called a hormone for the body to use. Different glands make different hormones

haemoglobin: the substance which makes blood red. Haemoglobin carries oxygen

haemophilia: a condition in which the blood is unable to clot

heart: the part of the body that acts as a pump to push blood around the body

heart attack: when the heart suddenly stops working as it should do

heart transplant: an operation in which a diseased heart is taken out and replaced with a healthy heart

hormone: a substance made in the body to trigger off changes such as growth. Hormones are carried around the body in the blood

humours: the four fluids which people used to believe were in the body. They were known as blood, choler, phlegm and melancholy

immune: when a person cannot catch a disease, because the body has built up the ability to destroy the disease as soon as it enters the blood

iron: a mineral substance that our bodies need to stay healthy

kidney: one of two parts of the body that cleans the blood by taking out wastes in the blood

large intestine: the second part of a long tube in which food is absorbed into the body and waste is pushed out

liver: a part of the body with many functions. The liver stores useful food parts, keeps the body at the right temperature and destroys poisons

lungs: the two sponge-like parts of the body used for breathing. Oxygen is taken into the body and waste gases are given out through the lungs

lymph: a colourless liquid which is made in the body. Lymph helps in cleaning the blood and fighting diseases

lymphatic system: fine tubes which carry a colourless liquid around the body

lymph node: places in the body where diseases and waste matter carried in a colourless fluid are destroyed, and the fluid is cleaned before it goes into the blood

microscope: an instrument that makes very tiny objects look a lot larger

muscle: a type of material in the body which can shorten itself to produce movement

nutrient: the part of any food which can be used by the body for health and growth

organ: a part of the body which has a particular job, such as the brain or stomach

oxygen: a gas found in air and water. Oxygen is very important to all plants and animals. We cannot breathe without oxygen

pacemaker: something in the body which sends out impulses to make the heart beat steadily. An artificial pacemaker can be used to correct a faulty heart

pituitary gland: a part of the body which sends out substances to control growth and other changes. The pituitary gland is found beneath the brain behind your forehead

plasma: clear yellowish part of the blood. Plasma is mostly water, and it carries the other parts of blood in it

platelet: a tiny particle in blood that helps make it thicken and clot

pressure: the action of something pressing on, or against, something else

pulse: a single beat of sound or light. The heart beats in a pulse, which we can feel at various points on our body

pulse rate: the speed at which your heart is working to pump the blood around your body. Your pulse rate increases when you do exercise

pus: a yellow liquid that is made when you get dirt and germs into a cut or wound. Pus is mostly made up of dead white blood cells

red blood cell: a part of the blood which carries oxygen

respiration: the way living things take in oxygen from air or water and get rid of carbon dioxide. Human respiration is by breathing air in and out

Rhesus factor: a substance found in some blood. Blood that does not have Rhesus factor cannot be mixed with blood that does

ribs: a series of long bones which form a cage around the heart, lungs and other organs of the chest

small intestine: the first part of the tube where food is absorbed into the body. It is a long coiled tube that leads from the lower part of the stomach

sternum: the long flat bone in the centre of your chest. Most of the ribs are attached to the sternum

stethoscope: an instrument that a doctor uses to listen to sounds in your body made by parts such as the heart and the lungs

thermometer: an instrument used to measure temperature

thyroid gland: the part of the body which sends out substances to control how the body uses energy. It is found at the front of the neck

thyroxin: the substance that controls how quickly food is used in the body

tissue: many cells in the body of the same kind joined together to do a particular job

transfusion: replacing unhealthy or lost blood with healthy blood

urea: a waste we get rid of in urine when we go to the lavatory

vaccination: giving someone a dose of specially treated germs that are not strong enough to give the person the illness, but strong enough for the body to learn how to protect itself against them

valve: a kind of flap which opens or closes to let a liquid pass in and out of a pipe or tube

vein: one of the main tubes that carry stale blood from all over the body, back to the heart and lungs

ventricle: one of two chambers in the lower part of the heart

villi: tiny finger-like parts inside the small intestine

virus: a kind of germ. Viruses are smaller than bacteria. They cause disease when they get inside the body's cells

vitamin: a substance found in some foods. Tiny amounts of vitamins are needed by our bodies for good health and growth

warm-blooded: describing an animal which can control its own body temperature. Humans are warm-blooded

white blood cell: a part of the blood that fights disease

Index